Contents

DEDICATION 2

CHAPTER 01: FORWARD 3

CHAPTER 02: GOODWILL 4

CHAPTER 03: GM JERRY C. PIDDINGTON 5

CHAPTER 03: HANSHI McCall's - FIND A WAY 13

CHAPTER 04: RICKY AND RANDY SMITH THE
GOLD DUST TWINS 29

CHAPTER 05: MASTER DOUG ARMSTRONG'S
BIOGRAPHY 44

CHAPTER 06 55

Article by…. 68

Avery King – August 19, 2014 68

Article by…. 68

Karate Magazine 68

MY LIFE 70

Marty Knight 79

DEDICATION

I would like to dedicate this book to my Hanshi Danny McCall. Hanshi McCall not only taught me how to fight, but he taught me how to live life. He taught me that the way you do anything, is the way you do everything, and with hard work

"EVERYTHING IS POSSIBLE, IF ONY YOU BELIEVE". (#Burn the Boat)

CHAPTER 01: FORWARD

American Style of Karate, called American Open Style, was established under the USKA sanctified charter established by O'Sensei Robert Trias, Father of American Karate. Our goal is to provide a martial arts organization that provides access to promotions, teaching credentials, honored titles, and proclamations of styles endorsed and signed by Grandmaster Jerry C. Piddington.

AKANA is committed to servicing its chartered schools and individual members by providing access to unique and established events, such as Tomoe Warrior, Kabuto Warrior, and Sun & Moon Tests, along with AKANA sanctioned tournaments, friendship competitions, seminars, and gatherings. AKANA members will join a network of like-minded martial artists from the West Coast to the East Coast who proudly wear the AKANA patch, representing something bigger than themselves for the greater good of all. We are a brotherhood of Karateka who strive to keep our art pure. But most of all, we are devoted to maintaining and honoring our rich heritage and prolific lineage with a genuine spirit of togetherness.

CHAPTER 02: GOODWILL

The Goodwill Career Center in Haywood County works closely with other community agencies and resources to provide professional employment services to local job seekers. They provide training and direction to show participants how to use various media as tools in their search for employment. Supplied with this knowledge, a new job seeker has a real place to begin a job search.

The center also provides services to local emergency and homeless shelters, along with scheduled visits to the local detention center. They connect participants with connections to access local resources for emergency food, housing, utilities, counseling, health care, and much more.

…written by Jeff Richardson and Ricky Smith

CHAPTER 03: GM JERRY C. PIDDINGTON

"Let us bring the spirit of our martial art ancestors into this new age through the American Karate Academies National Association for the greater gain of all. We can kindle our fire and transform our great heritage into greater achievements."

"And, in this corner, Jerry Piddington"... was the title of an article written about Mr. Piddington in the 1974 issue of Karate Illustrated Magazine, in which he appeared on the cover. Mr. Piddington was described in that article by his fellow karateka as one crazy dude, an animal even a crazy animal,that you needed a chair and a whip to fight. Piddington is a lifelong rebel who is still turning heads with his long hair and bushy beard, which earned him the nickname *The Untamed Lion*.

Blood and Guts Era

As a pioneer of American Sport Karate, Jerry Piddington traveled all over the country, placing or winning every major tournament in the United States from 1972 to 1976, not only in fighting but in kata competitions as well. Mr. Piddington faced off against some of the top tournament competitors of the 1970s - including Joe Lewis, John Natividad, Darnell Garcia, Bob Allegria, Steve Sanders, Jay T. Will, Artis Simmons, Joe Corley, Byong Yu, Ken Knudson, Everett Eddy, Roger Greene, Reily Hawkins, Jack Motley, Vic Guerro, Jeff Smith, and Pat Johnson, just to name a few. He began his competitive career in 1969, winning the Four

Seasons Karate Championships as a brown belt. He later captained the five-man team that triumphed over the highly successful Chuck-Norris-led team at the 1974 International Karate Championships in Long Beach, California. Mr. Piddington held a long list of titles over the years and in 1973 he was rated #9 in the USA, #1 in the Southeast by the Black Belt Yearbook, and #12 in the USA by Professional Karate Magazine. He participated in the Canada AM Championships and helped the American team defeat the Canadian team by scoring the winning point at 54 years old.

"I enjoyed fighting the bare-knuckle matches," says Mr. Piddington."In that era, the fights were much tougher because there were no pads and headgear. The art of kime and control with good stances was an important part of how we fought, unlike today's sport of karate of jump and tag." Mr. Piddington remembers some of his injuries, including a broken thumb at the

U.S. Team Championships in Long Beach, California; a broken jaw at Kang Rhee's Nationals in Memphis, Tennessee; and a broken leg at the 1973 Grand Nationals in Anderson, Indiana

Instructor Lineage

Mr. Piddington has a martial arts career that spans six decades and has studied with some of the most influential martial artists in the world. His first teacher was Caylor Atkins, a Shotokan stylist. Mr. Piddington received his first black belt from Tom Crites in Shorin-Ryu. Continuing his career, Mr. Piddington trained in Hawaiian Kenpo with Michael Stone, Japanese Goju-Ryu with Chris Armstrong, Kempo with Ed Parker, and Shorin-Ryu with Master Tadashi Yamashita. Mr. Piddington was also a student and friend of O'Sensei Robert Trias, the father of American Karate.

Movie Credits

Hanshi Piddington enjoys acting in live theater and stage combat. He has been a fight choreographer and stunt man in several major motion pictures, such as **Killer Inside Me, A Reason to Kill, Night Realm, The Quest,** starring Jean-Claude Van Damme and Roger Moore, and **BloodSport II,** starring Daniel Bernhardt, Pat Morita, and James Hong. He is currently filming a documentary and reality show based on his adventure to Cambodia called **When Two Masters Meet**

Pioneer of American Karate

Grandmaster Robert A. Trias took notice of Mr. Piddington and invited him to create the first American style of karate in the United States. On May 2, 1972, Mr. Piddington was declared the Headmaster and Founder of American Open Style Karate under the USKA sanctified charter, established by Master Trias, which was internationally ratified on May 30th, 1975. In February 2000, Mr. Piddington was declared Headmaster of American Shorei/Shorin Karate by Hanshi John Pachivas, Grandmaster of Shuri-yu Karatedo, and was awarded his 10th-degree black belt. Grandmaster Jerry Piddington founded the National Karate Association (NKA) in 1976, which evolved into the American Karate Academies. National Association (AKANA) in 1991.

Pioneer Promoter of Sport Karate and Kickboxing

In the 1970s, Mr. Piddington was one of the four promoters of Mike Stone's Four Seasons National Tournaments, along with Algene Caraulia, Pat Burleson, and Mike Stone. Mr. Piddington pioneered kickboxing on the East Coast by promoting five major kickboxing title fights in Charlotte, North Carolina. He was a co-writer with Joe Corley, establishing the rules for the Professional Karate Association (PKA), which are documented in the 1974 issue of Sports Illustrated. As

founder of the National Karate Association (NKA), Mr. Piddington promoted the first eleven-round world title kickboxing match with Jeff Smith winning a decision over Keith Haflick for the 1977 Light Heavy Weight Championship of the World with more than 5,000 paid spectators.

Founder of Tag Team/Five-man Team Kickboxing Championships

Also, under the NKA sanction, Mr. Piddington promoted the first World Double Pro Team (Tag Team) Kickboxing Championships with the Gold Dust Twins, Ricky and Randy Smith, defeating Dale Cook's team from Tulsa, Oklahoma, considered by many as some of the best kickboxing action to date. Mr. Piddington was also the founder of The Charlotte Warhawks, an undefeated five-man kickboxing team that included some of his most notable fighters: Danny McCall, Keith Haflick, Jimmy Horsley, Ricky Smith,

and Randy Smith. The team was coached by Danny Wilson and managed by Gene Smith.

Hall of Fames

Some of Hanshi's recent awards include:

- 2000 September: Inducted into the World Martial Arts Hall of Fame.
- 2002 August: Presented with the Living Legends Tiger Award by Chuck Norris in Burbank, California.
- 2003 October: Inducted into Living Legends as one of the greatest fighters alongside Joe Lewis, Jeff Smith, Don Wilson, Bob Wall, and Howard Jackson, in Charlotte, NC.
- 2013 August: Received the Joe Lewis Eternal Warrior Award, alongside Bill Wallace and Jeff Smith, at the Battle of Atlanta.
- 2014 August: Inducted into the Masters Hall of Fame alongside his teacher, Mike Stone, in Long Beach, California.
- 2017 July: Inducted into the Legends of Carolina Martial Arts as a pioneer of the art of sport karate in the Carolinas.

Spirit and Heart of a Lion

Jerry Piddington has been married to Eva Marie for over thirty years. He continues to teach American Open Style Karate at his dojo in Ashland, Oregon. His other passions are adventure-seeking sports such as high diving and extreme water sports. One of his highlights was river rafting the Tanna River in Alaska with class 5/6 killer rapids. He currently loves fishing and hunting. He is the father of three and the grandfather of four. Mr. Piddington has not only demonstrated the fighting spirit of a lion, but he continues to demonstrate the heart of a lion with his gift for working with kids who are educationally and physically challenged with ADD, ADHD, dyslexia, alcohol syndrome, autism, etc. Hanshi Piddington believes that the aesthetic value of martial arts can absolutely help kids by giving them a way of life.

Conducting AKANA Events

O'Shihan Jerry Piddington currently serves as Chief Advisor of AKANA, the organization he founded. There are 21 schools across the United States under its charter. Danny McCall, Ricky Smith, CJ Mayo, Randy Smith, and Joe McClellan are on the appointed board of directors. Hanshi Ricky Smith serves as director, Kyoshi Mayo as assistant director, and Hanshi McCall as senior advisor. O'Shihan travels across the United States and is currently available to conduct AKANA symposiums, seminars, gatherings, Tomoe Warrior Tests, Kobudo Warrior Tests, and Sun & Moon Tests to help improve any school's martial arts endeavors. If you would like to contact O'Shihan Jerry Piddington, you can reach him at mushinpower@hotmail.com.

CHAPTER 03: HANSHI McCall's - FIND A WAY

"IT IS POSSIBLE!" MARK 9:23

This is a small part of my book coming out at the end of next year, telling all about my Vietnam experience in detail and my Karate life and those who shaped it, including my desire to become an engineer and own my own business. I hope this inspires you to become the best you can be in life. Learn to be fearless, master yourself-serve others!!

As a small child, my first memories involved two subject matters. The first is looking up at a picture of Jesus on the cross in our living room. And the second was to learn later in life that I was adopted and my real mother lived only 2 streets away with my 4 stepbrothers (Ricky, Luke, Joe, and Andy Garcia). I never met my dad, and my real mom would call me to her death bed (she died of breast cancer) and give me the why? Then she would describe Mr. Garcia to me as an airborne ranger in the army at Fort Bragg. She did say he was the love of her life, but he was leaving to go overseas, and she never saw him again. My adopted parents were actually my aunt & uncle. They were very proud and God fearing and they named me Danny Ray McCall, which I always hated. But it was my name for life. I thought everyone went to church on Sunday, Monday, Wednesday and Saturday night. When I was 9 years old, I found out people would pay me to mow their yards. I started cutting grass all day on Saturday after I delivered the weekly morning paper. This was a real job, as they would drop the papers at 3:00 am and I would get my papers stuffed and bagged so I could deliver them before I went to school. My stepdad brought home a bike from the garbage (he was a garbage man), and it needed work, including a chain and a couple of tires. But to me, it was freed from rust. I went to the bicycle shop on Trade Street and got one item each week when I got paid, and before you knew it, I was mobile. I even got a basket for the front to be able to carry my papers. I was rich; I rode it to school and then to Grammas on Sunday after church. I felt like a true entrepreneur, riding around the neighborhood, offering my lawn services to anyone who needed them. I learned many valuable lessons during those early days of mowing lawns. First and foremost, hard work pays off. I would wake up early, deliver newspapers, go to school, and then spend the rest of the day mowing lawns. It was exhausting, but I saw the results of my efforts in the form of money in my pocket. I quickly realized that if I wanted something, I had to work for it. Another important lesson I learned was the value of savings. As my lawnmowing business grew, I started making more and more money. Instead of spending it all on toys and treats like most kids my age, I decided to save. I opened a savings account in a shoe box and made sure to deposit a portion of my earnings every week. This taught me discipline and the importance of planning for the future. Plus, no one knew where it was, under the floor. But perhaps the most significant lesson I learned was the power of determination and perseverance.

Then my stepparents had Ellen May, my half-sister. I was not their favorite child anymore since this was their little girl. The day she came home from the hospital, it was raining, and from that day forward, I would have to do for myself. My stepdad was drunk and when he came home, he sat around and thought up chores for me to do - cut wood and get the coal in when we needed it. My life would change forever since everything was about Ella May (named after Ella May from the Beverly Hillbillies), I loved her because she was awesome, and with blonde hair and blue eye, what was not to love?

I wanted to get my license to be a lifeguard. I told my parents, and they gave me the same motivational speech they always did."What do you want to do that for? You'll never be able to swim four times up and down that pool with your clothes on. You're too slow."

I had been swimming with Mike and Ralph late at night after everyone else left until Hub, their dad, found out and stopped it, unless I would work for the time I used the pool for free. I traded time in the pool for time in the snack shack (I could eat free there). I know it took me 9 months to a year, but I passed the lifeguard test and got a piece of paper that showed I was a certificated lifeguard. I told everyone, but I couldn't afford a tee shirt because it was 8 dollars. Finally, my stepmother gave me 5 dollars to get my red tee shirt, and I had 3 dollars saved back. It had Suttles Swimming Pool on the front and the big white letters "LIFEGUARD" on the back. I wore that shirt out from the inside since I got to sweep the pool, and the girls thought I was cool, so I wore it a lot. I kept the pool cleaner than anybody else.

The other memories were images of my stepfather's heavy hands. As I grew older, I realized that those hands became heavy, closed fists. Most of my friends at school would love for Friday afternoon to come. This meant the weekend. But, for me, it was a time of dread and anticipation of experiencing extreme abuse. My Christian faith had kept me going, during those violent beatings with fists, belts and tree branches I routinely received from my father. I was ashamed. I grew up distant and rebellious. My stepfather and I would have as little to do with each other as possible. My stepfather never even knew that I had played JV football. He did not know me. I only knew him during drunken rages, which started to occur several times a week.

At 15, I heard my father beating my mother. I hit him. He fell to the floor. He stood up, wiped the blood away from his lip, and said, "I was wondering when all this Badass crap would kick in.".He attempted to pull a knife on me. I kept fighting. He was much bigger than I was. One of his brothers (Bub) put me in a full Nelson. I escaped, took him to the floor, got up, and kept fighting my stepfather. I never really gave in; just waiting to leave someday.

I never graduated high school, and a couple months later I left my home to join the Army and attend U. S. Army Corps Boot Camp (a stricter dress code) at Fort Bragg, North Carolina. (I like to call it the University of Hell). This was to be the best education I had ever received. Those 8 weeks put a lot of muscle on my frame and helped shape my way of realistic thinking and a proper positive attitude for the rest of my life.

I got to travel to many, man, places. Vietnam is the most famous.

I was also lucky to train with many different people, from different systems of unarmed combat. I was an infantryman, but was sent to shake n bake school or non-commission offers school. Being there for 12 weeks, I would learn to be organized, disciplined, and respectful, before being shipped to Vietnam to be a Sergeant E-5 who was an 11D40, or Amory Reconnaissance Specialist Tank and Track Commander. Vietnam was an eye-opener. I arrived in Camron Bay, and it was so hot I could not breathe. I rode in a jeep to the huts and thought, well this is where I will die. While I was being processed, I looked at the board where I would be going and saw there was nothing but red. This meant it was a hot zone. I was assigned to H-Troop 17th Cav, 1st platoon, "the Wild Bunch." During that time, they told me to pull guard and then wash dishes since I was now a corporal. This happened after being busted from a Sergeant for going AOL in N.C. I never did anything but shoot pool, and I thought, "What the heck, what are they going to do? Send me to Vietnam?" So they can kiss it.

On June 7th, 1970, in the intense heat of Vietnam, I found myself stationed in Chu-Lai, my home base. We embarked on numerous missions, from combating the VC and NVA to providing road security on the treacherous roads spanning South to North Vietnam. The fateful day arrived when I would face the danger that awaited me. As the scorching sun began to descend, casting a cool breeze over the land, I assumed the role of lead APC track in our convoy (which means I was first in line leading the way), outfitted in only a flack jacket and Ho-Chi Minh sandals, and little did I know that, in the next five minutes, my life would be forever changed. Having been in the country for merely three months, the sudden chaos struck us like lightning. From two sides, the Viet Cong ambushed us, catching us off guard. I felt the impact of bullets piercing my knees and arms. In that moment, I saw my driver fall to the same fate, and the track spiraled out of control as rounds rained down upon us. Seeking safety within the APC track, I would drop down inside the track and crawl towards the driver. I mustered every ounce of strength to pull him away from harm's way, making sure that our track didn't plunge into the ambush unfolding around us. Blood soaked the interior of the APC, and amidst the chaos, my wounded gunner cried out for aid for his bleeding arm. The firefight seemed to stretch on endlessly, although I later learned it lasted only ten minutes. The loss of blood began to weaken me, but driven by determination and, praying, and making promises I keep to this day, I fastened a tourniquet around my leg and administered a dose of morphine. Though every second felt like an eternity, I held to in my mission to defend our team and myself.

My story is one of unwavering love for my fellow team of badasses who would have done the same for me. I went to the lengths I was prepared to go, even at the risk of my own life, for my team. Vietnam tested my faith, but it also ignited a fire within me — a fire that burns to this very day, reminding me of the sacrifices made by countless men and women who fought for the liberty and freedom we have.

Through the telling of my story, I hope to inspire others to recognize and appreciate the dedication of those who put everything on the line to protect the principles upon which our nation stands. Though the scars may remain, they serve as a reminder of the indomitable spirit that resides within each and every one of us, a spirit that propels me towards a future defined by unity, peace, and unyielding love for my country and family.

During my time in Vietnam, I had the privilege of serving alongside some extraordinary individuals. The bonds we forged in the face of adversity will forever shape my perspective on friendship and camaraderie. Although I kept to myself in the aftermath of my experiences, I eagerly volunteered for any opportunity to make a difference, to even the score, and to fight for the cause. As my remaining days dwindled to a mere 45, an unexpected chance arose. I was offered the position of a door gunner on a Huey helicopter, responsible for delivering much-needed supplies while escaping the hazards of the field. Without hesitation, I embraced the opportunity, eager to embark on this new chapter. However, the path ahead was far from a bed of roses. Over the course of countless hours and numerous engagements, I fulfilled my role as a door gunner. The missions were every day, the firefights intense, but the warrior burning within me propelled me to be the best on the M60. It was during this brief period that I earned the prestigious Air Medal, a testament to the challenges we faced and overcame. With approximately two weeks remaining in my tour, I sought a change of pace and requested to be assigned to the communication shack, known as the CQ, during the night shift. My responsibilities revolved around relaying crucial information to the right personnel and summoning assistance when necessary. I found peace and satisfaction in this role, successfully completing my final weeks as a NCO- CQ.

Having fulfilled my duty, I departed from the Army with the rank of Sergeant, a testament to my dedication and service. The recognition bestowed upon me for my combat actions included the Bronze Star, Silver Star, Air Medal, and Purple Heart. While each award holds significance, it is the sense of fulfillment within my heart that truly validates my contribution. Though my journey in Vietnam was marked by sacrifice and hardship, I firmly believe that I paid my part. In those harrowing moments, when life and death came together, I rediscovered the strength within me, granted a second chance by God, the higher power. The experiences, both triumphs and tribulations, serve as a constant reminder of the immense sacrifices made in the fight for freedom.

As I share my story with the world, it is my hope that others will come to recognize the unwavering dedication and commitment exhibited by soldiers and veterans. We fought not only for our country but for the ideals of liberty and justice that unite us all. May my journey serve as a testament to the resilience of the human spirit and the profound impact one person can have in the pursuit of personal growth & freedom.

The last part of this story is dedicated to Marsha Lynn McCall, who I started seeing in high school, was the smartest & most amazing lady you ever saw….I loved her, and we got married before I left for Vietnam. She was the only person to write me every day, and it took weeks to get a letter, and they were not usually in order. I figured she could use the money if something happened to me. If not for those letters she wrote me, giving me hope of what life would be like when I got home, I am sure I would not have made it. I learned a saying years later: "When there is faith in the future, there is power in the present!" We talked about living on the lake and our future, which kept me wanting to get it done and get home. Her mom had a house, and she sold it to us to help us get going. It was not easy for me, as I was having issues moving on and forgetting what I had done while in Nam. But at my first-year home, I had a few jobs. I did not like to be told what to do. So, I would quit. I always wanted to be an engineer, and Marsha said to use your VA and go to school…I tried working at night, but that never worked. I needed something to do, so I started taking Shotokan Karate with Paul Storms, and he also taught Judo. I loved it till I started watching kung Fu on TV. I wanted to learn it…so I found Joe Martin in 1974, and it was exactly what I needed. He was amazing with his skills as a smaller guy. But he could get it done. It was when we did the demos at Park Center and watch him wrestle a bear, that I knew this man had little fear. I would learn to catch arrows as part of the Demo and the Bed of Nails. I studied with him and determined to get a dragon & a tiger on my arms when I got my black sash. While training with Sifu Martin, I would learn to control myself and the feeling of my hate. I met Jerry Piddington, who came to town, and my life would change forever. He was a world champion and wanted to start a team to fight full contact. He taught me American Open-Style Karate & Kick Boxing. During my time with him, he offered me a job teaching Karate, and I said 'yes' if I could go to school and get my engineering degree. He said he would set up my schedule to do that. Last but not least, I soon tested for my black sash and my karate black belt on the same weekend. It was not easy; the first thing I did was fight Wally McGinnis for five 2-minute rounds before I started my kung fu test.

I did all my material and all 4 katas, which had over 100 moves in them. But then I sparred all 12 of the BB judges and, as I sat there thinking I had done a great job and no one hurt me and I only hurt a couple of them. I was soaking wet and it's about 7pm now after starting at 8:30AM,,,,,,,

I thought, "I DID IT". But I was told by my Sifu Martin I was too rough at times and had no compassion or humility when sparring and that I needed to take the next 9 months of probation to think about my actions. In my mind, "I HAD FAILED," but what Sifu taught me was - it's not how good you are or how bad you are, BUT can you control YOURSELF. I COULD NOT AT THAT TIME IN MY LIFE. Sure, I had won the fights but not with respect for those who could not keep up with my pace. Upon my reflection, I realize that I displayed excessive aggression during the test, which ultimately led to my failure. I acknowledge that this behavior was inappropriate and not in line with the principles and values of what Kung Fu Sifu Joe Martin taught me. I understand that Kung Fu is not just about physical strength but also about discipline, control, and respect & Honor. I failed to demonstrate these qualities during my test, and for that, I am truly sorry even to this day, but what a life lesson for me. I would like to assure you that I have committed to improving myself both physically and mentally every day of my life. I understand the importance of self-control and discipline in Kung Fu & Karate, and I have determined to work on these aspects of my training. I would be grateful for any guidance or additional training you have to provide to help me develop a better understanding of proper technique, control, and the values of Kung Fu after 50 years. I have continued to improve myself in the arts. Once again, I assure you that I did take this opportunity to learn from my mistakes and grow as a martial artist. It was the most humbling thing you could have done to me…. But,I moved on to be one who loved Karate while getting my engineering degree during that time and hopefully a better person in life because of my failure that day.

Thanks to Hanshi Piddington for his advice over the years about my temper and passion to win. The last 50 years have been amazing. My competition in the tournaments and full contact training and fights will be in my book coming out the end of next year, where I will tell it all. But I will list a little about my journey to date. (My book will go into these years working with JCP)

One of the first to pioneer the art of "Full contact karate" in North Carolina (1974) with my lifelong instructor, Jerry C. Piddington. He formed the "Charlotte War Hawks," who remained undefeated till they disband in 1979. It was then that I continued to fight on the point circuit for some 30 years. In that time, winning or placing in every tournament entered. I was one of the original founders of the DOJO organization in the early 70's.

In return for my loyalty to the Art and to Hanshi Piddington, I would work in the one of 5 dojos while going to college to get that engineering degree. Hanshi trained Hanshi McCall in all areas of fighting that included full Contact Karate, Sport Karate and Forms. The relationship resulted in Hanshi McCall becoming a NKA World rated Full-Contact fighter and one of Sport Karate's top fighters in the U.S. (with 100's of wins).

They pioneered the art of full contact fighting when the gloves were no more than ½ the weight of today's non-contact sport karate gloves - mere ounces, when a mouthpiece, hand wraps, and cup were optional, when spinning techniques and deadly blows were allowed. Hitting after the break was acceptable, as well as kicking while you were down and was even overlooked. Blood and guts don't even begin to describe the early wars in the full Contact Karate World.

Hanshi McCall, Martial Arts Instructor, administrator, and former World rated full contact fighter, holds an 9th Dan Black belt in American Open Shorei/Shorin Karatedo, 10th Dan in American Freestyle Karate (founded AFKD in 1975), a 4th Dan in Tae kwon Do, and a 1st Black Sash in Li Ki Kung Fu. He holds certifications as a Coach/Instructor, Referee, Rank Examiner and Kata Judge. Hanshi McCall has studied and trained with Grand Master Piddington for the last 47 years. Grand Master insured that Hanshi McCall trained with the best of the best, which included, Ross Scott, Joe Martin, Buddy Springs, Paul Storm, Parker Shelton, Glenn Keeney, Bill Wallace, Joe Lewis, Mike Genova, Bobby Tucker, Gary Lee, Ernie "Radar" Smith, Keith Vitali, Keith Haflich, Larry Hartsell, Ricky & Randy Smith and so many other great pioneers.

- Hanshi McCall is one of the Founding members of the American Karate Academies National Association. (AKANA)
- Living Legends Pioneer Award (2003) Hanshi & Bob Wall of World Black Belt.Com (co-star of "ENTER the Dragon" with Bruce Lee) awarded Kyoshi McCall the Living Legend Pioneer Award (2003).
- Kyoshi McCall was inducted as "Kyoshi of the Year" in the 2007 Universal Black Belt Hall of Fame in Texas July 2007.
- Hanshi McCall was inducted as "Golden Lifetime Achievement Award of Honor" in the World Karate Union Hall of Fame in Tanners, Pa., on June 28, 2008.
- Hanshi McCall was honored at the "2011 Dojo Organization Hall of Fame" as the "Greatest Heavy Wt. Fighters of his era.
- Hanshi McCall Awarded 2014 "Man of the Year" at the Dixie National Karate Tournament...by Dewey Earwood and members of the SC Karate BB Hall of Fame
- Hanshi McCall is a History General and Pioneer of American Sport Karate-Founder-Mr. Gary Lee

- Hanshi McCall was inducted into the Legends of the Carolina Martial Arts in 2017 and became a member of the Board of Director. Being selected by Brian Pena Founder and President of LCM

Hanshi McCall, owner of American Freestyle Karate Dojo of Denver, NC, received the PKA Joe Lewis Eternal Warrior Award in Atlanta,

Georgia on June 14 at the Battle of Atlanta 50-year anniversary karate tournament, held at the Renaissance Waverly Hotel and Convention Center. The inductees were selected from this 50-year span of sport karate history by promoter Joe Corley, along with martial art icons Bill Wallace and Jeff Smith. The reunion and banquet, called "The Gathering of World Changers", included karate and kickboxing champions who helped change the history of the sport. "These are the world changers of our sport," says Joe Corley. "They were the fighters willing to go one more round." This is the highest Fighters Award in the Martial Arts & PKA.

Hanshi McCall would Ventured to Sonora, Ca., (2007) to learn Firewalking from the Master Firewalking Instructor Tolly Burkan. Tolly Burkan is the most knowledgeable person in the world today on the art of Firewalking. Kyoshi McCall felt it was time for something new and choose to study and explore Firewalking. Kyoshi McCall became a certified Firewalking Instructor under Tolly Burkan. But only holds a Firewalk every 5 years……next one will be 2025. One of the most memorable Firewalk was on the grounds of Brian Pena's New Dojo locations. Sensei Pena would have a group of Who's Who in Columba, SC, to include the Mayor. This was in 2020, during the Pandemic and the riots in Columba. The Mayor would ask that we speed it up so he could walk on the Fire before the 10:00 O'clock Curfew. It was a great time for all to be part of the future of one of the finest Dojo's in the east.

Hanshi McCall started and operated Denver Recreational Marine, Inc in North Carolina (more on this in my book) and we grew into one of the largest Ranger Boat dealerships in the country. In 2000 was selected as the Dealership of the year. But after 30 years and two grand babies it was time to sell our dealership in 2017 to enjoy the Grandbabies & Life. Every Tuesday and Thursday and most Saturday Mornings, just like the last 50 years, you will find me teaching (or headed to the Beach). Along with Mr. McClellan and

Harvey Sharpe, son Matt McCall, David Washco, and Randy Sharpe. Ron Carroll runs a school in Shelby, NC and carries on our history. The Friday and Saturday classes are handled by Mr. Keever and Mr. Ward.

Mr. Lingerfelt and Mr. Godfrey handle the Fort Mill School after it was turned over in 1987, after Hanshi McCall had started the school in 1976.

These are some of the most dedicated and unselfish Black Belts who are true leaders and my FRIENDS. I have a chapter on each one of the 21 Black Belts I personally promoted over the last 50 years (more in my future Book about my Life).

Maybe it can encourage others to believe in their selves and become more than you ever thought possible. Mark 9:23:IT IS POSSIBLE!..............BURN THE BOATS....

In sharing a few chapters of my future book and Life story, I hope to convey the power of love, the resilience of the human spirit, and the transformative nature of finding one's true passion. Marsha and my deep love for her and the Family we have raised, intertwined with my journey into

the world of martial arts, became the catalyst for healing and personal growth. Together, we embarked on an extraordinary adventure, embracing life's uncertainties while cherishing the present and embracing the hope it holds for our shared future.

" WARRIOR'S PATH: A FATHER's JOURNEY THROUGH KARATE AND LIFE"

Check out www.mccallsamericankarate.com for more details!

"BECOME WHAT YOU BELIEVE" MATTHEW 9:29

Changed By Fire, Challenged by Life"

IT IS POSSIBLE! MARK 9:23

CHAPTER 04: RICKY AND RANDY SMITH
THE GOLD DUST TWINS

From China Grove, North Carolina

Ricky and his twin brother, **Randy**, from China Grove, North 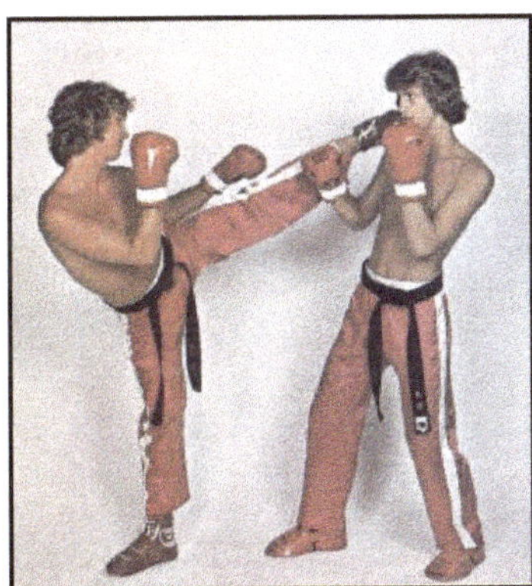 Carolina, were named The Gold Dust Twins by *Karate Illustrated* in 1977. Ricky was ranked 3rd in the United States and 10th in the World in Professional Kickboxing. The highlight of Ricky and Randy's exciting career came in 1978, when the duo won the Double Pro-Team (Tag Team) Kickboxing Championship of the World, sanctioned by the National Karate Association. This fight is still considered by many as one of the most action-packed bouts in the history of Full-Contact Karate. The twins also fought as super-lightweights for the world famous undefeated five-man kickboxing team, The Charlotte Warhawks, alongside Danny McCall, Jimmy Horsley, and the late Keith Haflich.

Randy had an extremely powerful straight right hand punch and was properly named The Bullet. Ricky had lightnin- fast hand and foot combinations and was nicknamed Flash after knocking out his first opponent in a record-setting seventeen seconds. The  Gold Dust Twins were two of the most colorful and popular fighters of their era. *(Randy is pictured above performing a roundhouse kick on Ricky - 1977)*

Ricky and his wife, Edie, currently own SideKick Karate of Salisbury, North Carolina. In 1975, Ricky and Randy opened their first karate school in China Grove, North Carolina, and began their teaching career. The twins are founders of SideKick Karate and have produced hundreds of black belts. Some of their most notable current teachers are Robert Taylor (8th Dan), Jeff Dixon (6th Dan), Madison Hobbs (4th Dan), and Shawn Bolick (3rd Dan). Ricky and Randy are founders of the American Open Karate System and Ricky is the current director of the American Karate Academies National Association (AKANA) founded by Hanshi Jerry C. Piddington. *(Ricky is pictured on the right, performing a flying side kick on Randy.*

Ricky and Randy had the honor of studying and ranking under some of the best karate teachers and competitors in the history of martial arts, including Jerry C. Piddington, Robert H. Bowles, the late Ridgely Abele, Troy Price, the late Vitus Bilking of Denmark, the late legendary Joe Lewis, David A. Adams, and the late Gary Basinger.

Their first karate teacher was Gary Basinger *(pictured on the left in the center of Randy and Ricky - 1975)*. The twins joined Gary's school in 1974 and traveled the sport karate circuit for years under his tutorship, racking up wins all over the Southeast. "Gary was one of the best sport karate competitors, with more grand championship trophies than anyone I know," said Randy.

In 1976, the twins received their first black belt from David A. Adams, a pioneer of karate in the Southeast. The brothers also began their full-contact karate profession under his leadership. In the next few years, Dave coached the twins to a top ranking kickboxing career as they fought some of the best kick boxers of their era, including world champions Tony Lopez, Richard Jackson, and Vernon Mason. Ricky and Randy currently hold 9th degree black belts in American Jee Do Kwan under Mr. Adam's American Jee Do Kwan Association. In 2005, the twins also starred in one of Dave Adams' films, ***Angel with a Kick***, along with the late martial arts legend, Thomas C. LaPuppet.

In 1977, the Smith Brothers began training American Open Style Karate under Hanshi Jerry C. Piddington and developed a student-teacher relationship that has lasted to this day. Ricky and Randy are 9th degree black belts in American Open Karate under the AKANA banner. Ricky and Randy are also 5th degree black belts under Joe Lewis in his American Karate Systems *(pictured on the left in the center of Ricky and Randy)*. "Joe was 52 years old when we had to spar him three rounds for our 5th degree black belts," said Randy. "My dad paid for the promotions for our 36th birthday so he could watch us get knocked around," added Ricky with a laugh. Ricky is also a 2nd degree black belt in Shuri-te Bujutsu under Troy Price. Ricky and Randy have 5th degree black belts signed by the late John Pachivas. Ricky also has rank in White Crane Fist Style under O'Sensei Robert Bowles.

The Gold Dust Twins' accomplishments have not only been in competition but teaching. In 1994, the twins were inducted into the World Martial Arts Hall of Fame as Instructors of the Year and Ricky also won the Kata Grand Championship in the World Martial Arts

Hall of Fame Tournament that year

(Pictured to the right). "We feel that we received our passion for teaching from our mother, who was a 12th grade English teacher for thirty-four years," said Ricky.

As promoters of sport karate, Ricky and Randy have promoted kickboxing and karate tournaments since 1981. Their televised kickboxing productions, held in China Grove, North Carolina, included some of the best fighters in history of the sport, such as Bill "Gentleman" Morrison, Johnnie "Superfoot" Davis, and the infamous Joe Lewis. In 2003, Ricky and his wife decided to give back to the martial arts community by honoring some of the great legends of sport karate. They promoted Living Legends of Sport Karate in Charlotte, North Carolina, honoring the world's greatest fighters of all-time, including Jeff Smith, Jerry

Piddington, Don "The Dragon" Wilson, Bob Wall, Joe Lewis, and Howard Jackson.

In the same event, Ricky and Randy were inducted into the Sport Karate Museum as Living Legends of Sport Karate. Their father, Gene, was honored with the Living Legends Pioneer Award *(pictured on the left from left to right - Randy, Gene, Bob Wall, and Ricky).*

In 2017, Ricky and Randy were inducted into the first class of Legends of Carolina Martial Arts. A pinnacle of The Gold Dust Twins' career was in 2018, when they received the Joe Lewis Eternal Warrior Award by Bill Wallace and Jeff Smith. The award was given to the top 50 fighters in America by the Professional Karate Association (PKA).

Ricky and his wife have given back to their community by founding and promoting The Bushido Warrior Sparring Tournaments with special guests such as Bob Wall and Howard Jackson. In a ten year span, the event raised over $100,000 for Godstock, a local organization that helps families with critically ill children. The Smiths are still promoting annual karate tournaments through their SideKick Karate Schools.

Ricky and Randy also have a love forfilmmaking and a vision for martial arts films made for family entertainment with a Godly message of hope. Their film resume includes: **Angel with a Kick** - a 2005 Dave Adams Film starring Thomas LaPuppet with Ricky and Randy Smith, **The Quest** - A 1996 Universal Picture starring Jean-Claude Van Damme and Roger Moore, in which Ricky was a stuntman and portrayed a pirate *(pictured on the left with Jean-Claude Van Damme)*, ***Bloodsport II: The Next Kumite*** - A 1996 FM Entertainment Production starring Pat Morita (Mr. Miyagi) and Daniel Bernhardt, in which Ricky portrayed a fighter in the Kumite *(pictured below with Jerry Piddington on the left and Mr. Miyagi in the center)*, and ***The Russian Godfather*** - A Hollywood Star Entertainment Production starring Jeff Conway which Ricky and Randy were stuntmen and portrayed bodyguards.

Ricky and Randy are the authors of a Volume I, II, and III series of karate books. The first hardback edition, ***American Open Karate System***

Illustrated Training Manual, will consist of 650 pages with over 6,500 drawings illustrating every technique in American Open Karate. Ricky and Randy have worked on this project since 1979. "This book is our legacy to American Open Karate and a gift to my teacher, Hanshi Jerry Piddington," adds Ricky. Ricky and Randy have also produced several martial art training videos with Side Kick Karate Productions. Their first instructional video, ***Get Started in Karate***, was endorsed by Joe Lewis and Jerry Piddington in the introduction. Also, they produced an instructional video, ***Living Legends Sport Karate and Kickboxing Seminars***, featuring four of the greatest legends in karate and kickboxing history: Joe Lewis, Don Wilson, Jeff Smith, and Howard Jackson.

Ricky and Randy grew up at their dad's 43-acre recreational park, Happy Lake. They began to lifeguard and learn work ethics at an early age. Randy pursued a 20-year career with Lack's Beach Service, managing ocean rescue and water safety in Myrtle Beach, South Carolina. He received the 1997 Rookie of the Year Award and was honored with the 2009 Carl D. Righter, Jr. Horry County Beach Front Veteran Meritorial Service Award.

In 2018, Ricky and Randy received their Headmaster of American Open Karate System certificates from Mr. Piddington, endorsed by some of the most notable pioneers of the martial arts, including Chuck Norris, Robert Bowles, Pat Burleson, Roy Kurban, Jeff Smith, Bill Wallace, Dennis Brown, Joe Corley, and Dan Inosonto. In 2023, Ricky received his Hanshi title for AKANA, endorsed by O'Shihan Jerry C. Piddington and O'Sensei Robert H. Bowles.

In 1989, Ricky and Randy gave their hearts to Jesus and began to serve God. Ricky traveled with a well-known youth evangelist, Eastman Curtis, out of Lakeland, Florida, and Randy served as a youth pastor in Tallahassee, Florida. In 1991, Ricky and Randy founded the Double Impact Ministry Team, using their martial arts demonstrations as a tool to reach the youth of America. The twins continue to use their martial arts platform to preach the gospel through their SideKick Karate Black Belt Ministry. "The highlight of our week is busing the SideKick Karate kids to church every week," says Ricky.

In 2017, Ricky and Edie developed an after-school/summer camp program which expanded into servicing over seventeen schools with four buses throughout Rowan County. In 2018, Ricky and Edie implemented a martial arts program through the Salisbury/Rowan School System, teaching "atrisk" kids. It has a statistical success rate of forty-seven percent of the students improving their behavior and grades.

You can visit Ricky and Randy's website at www.sidekickdojo.com or email them at skkarate@aol.com.

Chapter 4: *"A journey of a thousand miles, begins with one footstep."*

My name is James Cooper, and this is my story about Karate. My story began in my early 20's, when it was at the Run-Bu-Kun School of Karate. My first instructor was Randy Patterson. The style Randy taught was Shotokan Karate. My classes were very positive but very disciplined. My instructor was a great role model and he made me believe in myself. I also learned that everything is possible if you believe in Christ. In addition to this, I learned that you can do anything you set your mind to. Today, as I look back, Proverbs 23:7 comes to mind: "What a man thinketh in his heart, so he is". This was the beginning of an amazing journey that would take me places that I had never thought possible, and help me to realize that "how you do anything is how you do everything". My story is one of ups and downs, but as I look back, I realize that all hard work leads to profit, but mere talk leads to poverty, and everything is possible if only you believe.

Not long after this, I moved to Lenoir, N.C. where my karate training would really take off. I enrolled as a student at Winkler's Karate in Granite Falls, N.C., where I had the pleasure of meeting Robert Winkler, my new teacher and mentor. The first thing I was taught, was that Karate was not for the bragger or the

boastful, and that "you can do anything you set your mind to do, whether you think you can or can't, you are probably right". I was taught that you must be willing to do today what other people will not do in order to have tomorrow, what other people do not have, and that service to many, leads to greatness. There I started out as a white belt and would go through the ranks to get my black belt. This is where I became involved in competition. It started out as Point Karate and quickly moved into full contact Kickboxing. I was taught that "all hard work leads to profit but mere talk leads to poverty". There I was taught the true meaning of hard work. My first full contact fight was in Asheville for the Western Carolina Championship, which I won by decision. This helped me with my self-confidence and helped me to believe in myself, and "can't" is a four-letter word.

I started my career off with a fight in Asheville, N.C. for the Western Carolina Kickboxing title. I remember it like it was yesterday. I remember the feeling I got when I won for the first time. It made me feel like I had done something very special. "Failure is not failure, but only a learning experience." I remember when I was a student at Winkler's Karate. I would practice my Katas in my backyard along with my 7-P's every day. It was there that I was taught that the way you do anything is the way you do everything. While practicing over and over, I actually made a mud hole in my backyard (LOL). You must be willing to do today what others won't do in order to have tomorrow what other people don't have. I was very successful in the local tournaments. This is where I met the famous Dillingham Brothers. It was then, I decided that I was going to become a Black Belt, no matter what. I started training night and day! it was time for me to get off the bench and get into the game. The journey had begun and it would be difficult, but I knew I had what it took to become a better version of myself.

I was very active in all the tournaments in the area. Before long, I got my first experience in full contact Karate. During these tournaments, I met Arthur Ferguson and Roger Jones. I was actually able to train with Arthur, better known as "Star Child."

During my training, I was taught that "fatigue makes cowards of us all". I started running and working-out on the heavy-bag and sparring on a regular basis, discovering that I could do anything if I set my mind to do it. The sky was the limit! I was moving up through the ranks of American Karate. "Superior mind, superior body, superior attitude; each new challenge builds strength and charter".

(L to R) Robert Muse, Kenny Cooper

Denver Karate Club Students Win Honors

It took me five years to achieve my first black belt, and I must say that "I did not just get it, I grew into it." Not long after that, I moved to Denver, N.C. It was there that I met Hanshi Danny McCall. He taught me the true meaning of Karate. Hanshi McCall was a former Kickboxing Champion, and it was there that I was taught that you should always be devoted to your commitment, and that there are three aspects of Karate;" Superior Mind, Superior Body, and Superior Attitude."

Hanshi McCall, James Cooper, Kiyoshi Joe McClellan

<u>**School Pledge**</u>

"KARATE"

K IS FOR KNOWLEDGE

A IS FOR ATTITUDE

R IS FOR RESPECT

A IS FOR ABILITY,

T IS FOR TRAINING

E IS FOR EFFOR

<u>**"CREED OF A CHAMPION"**</u>

"I am not judged by the number of times I fail, but by the number of times I succeed, and the number times I succeed is in direct proportion to the number of times I fail, and keep on trying."

It was with Hanshi Danny McCall that I learned the Five Failures, and as I look back, I realize that they would not only help me in karate but in everyday life as well. My training has become a way of life for me and Hanshi Danny McCall and I have become lifelong friends. Hanshi Danny not only taught me the true meaning of Karate, he also taught me a lot about life. We began going to a large number of tournaments, and Hanshi Danny would line me up with plenty of full contact fights. I decided I would be a champion and failure was not an opinion! Hanshi Danny taught me how to "plan my work and work my plan."

<table>
<tr><td><u>THE FOUR ELEMENTS OF</u></td><td><u>KARATE</u>
<u>FIVE ANIMALS OF KARATE</u></td></tr>
<tr><td><u>1. SPEED:</u></td><td><u>1. Dragon</u></td></tr>
<tr><td><u>2. POWER</u></td><td><u>2. Tiger</u></td></tr>
<tr><td><u>3. TECHNIQUE</u></td><td><u>3. Leopard</u></td></tr>
<tr><td><u>4. BREATHING:</u></td><td><u>4. Crane</u></td></tr>
<tr><td></td><td><u>5. Snake</u></td></tr>
</table>

What I did not know at the time, was that Hanshi Danny was turning me into a teacher, and soon I would be starting a school of my own.

I decided to move to Newton-Conover, where I rented an up-stairs apartment on Main Street to use as my Dojo and living space. It was in bad shape, but I knew that everything was possible, if only you believe. After leaving work one afternoon, I returned to my apartment, where my students had painted the Dojo

and the room where I had been living. This was a real blessing to me. It was hard at first, but I was determined, and soon this would wind up being a good success story. I simply practiced my 7-P's, ate right, slept right, and got to work on time. My school grew like a weed and soon I outgrew the Dojo on Main Street and would be moving to the Food Lion Shopping Center in Conover, N.C. "The bet was yet to come!" I had a friend at work who wanted me to meet his son-in-law. His name was Doug Armstrong, the soon to be World Champion Doug Armstrong! Doug and I would soon become good friends and soon after that, I met Robert "The Dragon' Walton. Doug and I would meet at my Dojo on the nights that I did not have classes and help train Robert for his upcoming, Hickory Bad Man Contest. Doug would spar with Robert, who was 6'-5", and weighed in at to 265 pounds! Robert would go on to win the Bad Man Contest. During this time, Doug and I became very good friends. We were walking by faith and not by sight; we were unstoppable. Not long after that, Doug would start teaching his own classes at my Dojo. When I look back, I was planting a seed that would grow into what is now known as Mountain View Karate Center in Hickory, N.C., and Doug would go on to become a world champion and have over 100 Black Belts. Twenty years later he has the biggest and best school in the Hickory area. I was very successful and was able to help a lot of people there. I was taught to be the champion of others. I was there for five years and I am so thankful for the time I spent there and the relationships I built during that time. "To God be the glory, show me your ways o-Lord teach me your path." Well, they say you always wind up back home, and I am no exception to the rule. I would move back home and start a school at Waynesville Parks and Recreation, but the name of my Dojo did not change, it was still "The LAST DRAGON SCHOOL OF KARATE" and Karate had become my destiny.

Proverbs 23.7 "What a man thinketh in in his heart, so he is."

Psalms 1:3 – *"And he shall be like a tree planted by the rivers of water, that bringeth forth his fruit in his season; his leaf also shall not wither; and whatsoever he doeth shall prosper."*

CHAPTER 05: MASTER DOUG ARMSTRONG'S BIOGRAPHY

1964- Douglas Allen Armstrong 9lbs 11oz. is born in Rochelle Illinois to Lee Allen and Elizabeth (Betty) Joann Armstrong on February 12th. Abraham Lincoln's birthday.

1964-1983 Grew up and lived in Oregon Illinois with my older brother and sister, Greg and Diane Armstrong

1981-1982: I started martial arts career at the age of 17 with my best friend Gerald Lint's. We trained with Master Sam an in the art of ji-do-kwon tae-kwon-do, in Byron, Illinois. Currently, Sam an resides in Rockford, Illinois. His karate school has approximately 400 students, with me being one of his first students. Competed in my first large tournament. 2nd in forms 1st in fighting

1982: Graduated Oregon High School

1983- Left for the U.S Navy June 30th

1984-1985: trained with Master Joseph Bunch in the art of

Okinawan-Kenpo-karate while stationed in Pearl Harbor, Hawaii.

1987-1990: trained with Sensei Dean Bottomley in the art of Shinjimasu-shaolin-goju. Competed in dozens of tournaments in Hawaii as an under belt. Our team had quite a reputation as being serious business. The tournaments in the islands in the late 80's were giant. Earned my Shodan (1st Degree) in 1990.

1989: trained with Grandmasters Wally Jay, Professor U.R.L.anka, Raymond Tabosa, Les Anyos, and Charles Dixon.

1990: Moved from Hawaii to Hickory, North Carolina, After Marrying Navy girl Pam Armstrong.

1993: Daughter "Brooke Alynn Armstrong" is born in October.

1992-1994:Taught for Sensei James "Kenny" Cooper at his Shotokan dojo (Conover, NC)

1995: Trained the Hickory Tough man Champion, Robert Walton. With Help from my friend Kenny Cooper at his dojo. Kenny was a veteran full contact fighter.

1996:April 8th Opened Mountain View Karate Center founded my own style of American Ching-Sai-Do (combined martial art), a combination of small circle jiu-jitsu, goju, taekwondo, grappling, and lots of breaking. Taught Three nights a week and worked full time as a cable contractor

1997:Daughter "Holli Eva Armstrong" is born in July. Named after Hale'iwa beach (pronounced- Holly Eva) on the North Shore of Hawaii, where her mom (pam) and I lived.

1999:started teaching full time, ranked first two students to black belt- Terry Maynard and Jerry Duncan.

1999: Seriously injured on August 6th being shocked working cable T.V. at the top of telephone phone pole and falling. Landing on the asphalt broke my pelvis in two places, among many other serious injuries.

2000: Won adult black belt Dojo Organization Fighter of the Year for the southeast.

2000: Won NBL world title in the breaking competition.

2001: Trained first students to world titles-Jerry Duncan and Rachel Maltba

2006-was promoted to sixth dan by 9th degree Hanshi Dean Bottemley.

2010: Adopted Soledad Estrada. A 16-year-old black belt of mine who was in need. She is one of the best humans on the earth.

2013: Was promoted to seventh dan by my peers, including: Magic Johnson, Garry Dillingham, Preston Rodgers, Charles Burris, Ray Rice, Maurice Moore, Ricky Taylor, Johnny Watkins, and my Instructor, Hanshi Dean Bottomley.

2017- Out of 3000 students that have trained at Mountain View Karate Centers, I have promoted 81 black belts. I currently have 10 black belts that are active in the dojo, and 3 that are on the payroll. Our karate team, Team MVKC, has ranked in the top 25 in the world, four different years including #24 last year. The Mountain View Open (hosted by MVKC) has been the largest sport karate tournament in North Carolina in the last 10 years.

2019- Met my love Deborah Abigail Alonso (D.A.A like me. :) Positive points- Master at coloring hair and stylist, cooking, comedian, leading, beauty and mom. Also, my best friend.

2021- Currently have ranked 96 black belts. Also ranked two world champion friends and team M.V.K.C. members Johnny Watkins and Mike Cunningham to 6th degree due to accomplishments and they no longer had active instructors.

2022- Son "Captain Douglas Armstrong" is born in February. First Armstrong boy in 57 years since I was born.

* Have taught dozens of breaking seminars to hundreds in the south east.

*M.V.K.C. has been the #1 south eastern sport karate breaking school since 2002

*Trained 47 world champions since 2001

*Ranked to 8th degree black belt on August 26th, 2017, by Grand Master Dean Bottomley

Some if my philosophies include-

"There is only one real Master"

"Success is in preparation"

"Tough times don't last, tough people do"

"The more you sweat in peace, the less you bleed in battle"

"Do not dwell on your mistakes, learn from them and go on"

"Anything is possible if you put your mind to it"

"A bad word about someone is better off left unsaid"

"Be nice. Until it's time not to be nice"

"Showing respect, earns respect"

"It's better to be judged by 12 than carried by six"

Testimonial

In the late 60"s growing up in a small town of 3500 people, religion was not a big thing, as I was never taught much about God. We prayed before Thanksgiving dinner but that was about it. My grandmother, Ruth Armstrong, went to Sunday school a few times. There was a lot of hard work from my parents and our house was spotless, but the weekends involved a lot of drinking, late nights and my parents who were outstanding, had a lot of huge arguments. Al and Betty were married 47 years until I lost my mom to smoking in 2003. Then I lost my true mentor, my dad, in 2006.

I dabbled off and on with religion a little until August 6th when I was working 60 hours a week installing cable TV and teaching karate three nights a week. I was doing a regular trap installation at the top of a telephone pole, and I received part of a 12000-volt shock. The electricity held me in place for a couple seconds, trying to kill me. I was not ready to leave this earth yet and managed to slip my foot off of the ladder rung. I fell approximately 22 feet. Landing on my right rear end, breaking my pelvis in two places, along with other serious injuries. Hitting the ground also knocked the wind out of me worse than any other time I had ever experienced in martial arts. There was no one around. I crawled to the tailgate of my truck and waited. My phone was broken so I couldn't call for help. I finally saw someone walking and I got their attention. Eventually, an old ambulance arrived and took me on the roughest, most painful ride I've ever taken.

During my 8-day stay in the hospital, I had 94 visitors who

checked on me. At one time I was on pain medicine, and I had everyone laughing so hard that the nurses limited me to three visitors at a time. This was because we were disrupting the other rooms with noise... I had some very influential and upstanding visitors, including pastors and the mayor of Hickory, N.C. A few of my friends and pastors had me pray with them and one gifted me with a Bible. It was at this point in my life that I turned over a new leaf and put my life in God's hands since he decided to give me a 2nd chance. I was so thankful to the Lord because I had a wife and two beautiful daughters, and he was looking out for us all. This was when I realized God, family, and health trump any other things in life. While lying in the hospital one late night by myself, I vowed to get back into serious competition. The rest is history.

I believed God steered me down the path of helping and training people and children the rest of the time he blessed me with on this earth. After all, he decided I could stay. August 6th was the last real job I've ever had. Thanks to God, he has allowed me to do something I love and have a lifelong passion for. Hopefully, I have changed some lives for the better. I am a happy and more complete man. Thanks be to God.

Kenny Cooper has always been a great friend I can count on and made me realize I had an open door to the Kingdom of God.

"Martial artists are more respected; stick with the arts"

"With God all things are possible" Matthew 19:26

Sincerely,

Master Hanshi Douglas Allen Armstrong

8th Jan

Founder, Soke of American Ching Sai Do

828-446-1477

Guest speaker, Preston Rodgers Banquet

I am here today to pass down some knowledge that will hopefully affect you in a positive way in your martial arts journey.

I want to thank Grand Master Preston Rodgers for allowing me to be the guest speaker.

Preston and I met in 1995 and have always been there for each other ever since. He has been at all 22 Mt. View Open tournaments and judged at all my East Coast sparring championships. I always say, "A black belt is only as good as their word" and "if you say you're going to do something, do it right". Great black belts follow this code of honor, and Preston is one of the best.

Master Rodgers demands 100% effort from every student he has ever trained, and he firmly believes that anything worth doing is worth doing right. That goes with everything in life. Whatever you choose to do, take the extra time to do it correctly.

Judging Master Rodgers' Team Tae Kwon Do for so many years has been my honor. Team members are talented, skilled, dedicated, loyal, tough, and most importantly, respectful.

Being humble is a huge part of martial arts. Preston, Garry, Johnny, Sushi, and Carrie are some of the humblest people I have ever had the privilege to know. They, and many others present today, truly exemplify what it means to be humble. The best doesn't say they are the best. Others say it for them if they really deserve it.

A great master taught me long ago about the 5 self's….

1) Self-respect

2) Self discipline

3) Self Confidence

4) Self control

5) Self Defense

That outstanding man was Master Preston Rodgers!

Master Doug Armstrong

Some if my philosophies include….

- "Success is in preparation."

- "Tough times don't last, tough people do."

- "The more you sweat in peace, the less you bleed in battle."

- "Do not dwell on your mistakes, learn from them

and go on.”

- “Anything is possible if you put your mind to it.”

- “A bad word about someone is better off unsaid.”

- “Be nice. Until it’s time not to be nice.”

- “Showing respect, earns respect.”

- “It’s better to be judged by 12 than carried by six.”

- “Martial artists are more respected.”

- “Stick with the arts,”

Joe Corley, James Cooper, Doug Armstrong

CHAPTER 06

My name is Mike Cunningham. I started martial arts in 1969, when it wasn't even cool like it is now. Neil Armstrong had just landed on the moon. At the age of six, I feared my own shadow.

(Isaiah 41:10: - Do not fear for I am with you; be not despaired; I am your God; I will help you; I will uphold you with my righteous right hand.")

I was easy prey for schoolhouse bullies. I took all their rants, raves, slurs, and bullying and turned them into positive energy to become the Christian martial artist I am today. But still, the enemy kept telling me that I couldn't. I wasn't good enough; I wasn't strong enough.

(Mark 9:24, "I believe forgive my unbelief.")

Martial arts allowed me to have the confidence to conform my body and my mind to do things I never really thought I could. I had a slow start in martial arts, but achieved black belt status in taekwondo in 1980. Achieved 2nd black belt in American karate style called curacao under Master Instructor Keith Allen, 9th Dan, in 1985. I tell students all the time that fighting is not what martial arts is all about. It's about being able to recognize your surroundings and determine whether there is an intimate threat at hand or not. Always be nice until it's time not to be nice. One of the reasons I like karate tournaments so much is that each opponent is basically at the same level, height, and it's a fair competition, unlike the real world, where people can hurt anyone without guilt or remorse. We are all God's children. I have competed in hundreds of competitions all over the United States. If memory serves me correctly, I competed with the author of this book, James Cooper, in 2000. Which, by the way, is one of the fastest fighters in his generation. God has blessed me with great traditional instructors such as Keith Allen, Arthur Ferguson, and Jim Richards. It took me 11 years to reach black belt. Much time, commitment, and dedication to classes and repetition are needed to learn the katas and history. Commitment to practice at home and repetition, repetition, and more repetition. Then I started doing what all instructors do: teaching and passing on knowledge.

(Psalm 46: 1-0, "Be still and know that I am God.")

Becoming a black belt takes much time and commitment and does not happen overnight. For every 10,000 students that start martial arts, only one will make it to black belt. There is no set timeline that can be given nor predicted for obtaining the black belt level. As each step of the way is determined by amount of time, practice, and commitment put forth and each student is different. There's a Chinese proverb that says, "When student is ready, the sensei will appear." Once black belt is achieved, you can earn degrees 1 through 10, called dans. They are earned by giving back, teaching others, and further testing. Dedication, devotion, and service. God blessed me with great health and strength

early on and I felt I I could do more. So, I prayed for God's guidance and I was able to be blessed to be a member of Team MVKC in 2001. I had a great sport karate coach, Doug

Armstrong, who fine-tuned me for competitions and ultimately helped me achieve my goal of winning a sport karate world title. I wanted to get a world title in breaking before I was 40. The first time, I went out to Hollywood, California and competed and received runner-up to World Champion Dann Baker. I still had another couple years to compete and in 2002, 1 was blessed to win almost every breaking event I competed in that year. I was given the number one seat in the Eastern United States.

(Isaiah 46: 1 0, "Be still know that I am God." When doubt came, God referred me back to his word, "Be stil, Michael." God says, "Anything is in your grasp if only you believe.")

The World Games were held by the National Black Belt League Super Grands in Panama City, Florida. I went with my team coach, Doug Armstrong, myself, and my man, Jerry Duncan, who was competing for junior division breaking. I was so nervous, and I knew this was probably going to be the last time I competed professionally. I was going against some of the toughest breakers in the world. Getting ready, I was praying God would give me a sign. I want to give special thanks to the late great Tammy Zimmerman.

(John 14:14, "Ask anything in my name and I will do it.")

I wanted this so bad. I had trained my whole life to get to this one point. I knew God loved me and has carried me through the many trials this life has had to offer. I was getting ready to compete and Tammy said, "Mike, look at me, it's within your grasp." God reminded me to ask anything in his name and he will do it. I got out there suddenly, and a calmness came over me that I'd never experienced in my life. I was at total peace. At the end of the division, I was blessed with the sport karate 2002 world title, a 1 0 carat gold ring and a NBL first-place black belt. Martial Arts may not be for everyone, but as I tell people, it's not all about the fighting. It's easy to hurt someone; what's hardest is to love them. Which is what God desires us to do. I have had many students over the years and when my youngest son, Keith Cunningham (shown in the -photograph here), obtained a first-degree black belt.

This was a very emotional day for a father to see his son fall into his footsteps. A surprise blessing was on the same day I was promoted to 6th Dan black belt and we received certificates the same day, father, and son. Love and respect Sheehan Mike Cunningham 6, Dan black belt

I was invited to take "Totally Christian Karate" by my cousin, and I thought, "I can't do that"! It was expensive, but fortunately there were scholarships available through my cousin's church. I decided to enroll my son, and every time I watched him practice, it seemed to help him with his Bible studies, which were part of his belt advancement. The more I saw him train, the more I wanted to be part of it. So, I prayed, and the Lord made a way for both of us to take

classes. Our instructor made a separate class for "us ladies" (my cousin, myself, and two other amazing women), one of which I graduated high school with. This was a life-changing journey for me! This lady that I had graduated with, I had known since elementary school. She had bullied me and looked down on me because "she had more and better things than I had." We were poor in all aspects of life, but my mother always made a way for us to have what we needed and kept her faith even as a single mom. I had hatred in my heart when I saw this old high school colleague, but she ran and hugged me and told me she was so glad to see me and that she loved me, and I thought, "Really, do you remember me really". As we started this journey together, I found out that she had been bullied too. She had been a popular cheerleader, with great clothes and natural beauty. She had it all, "I thought," but she had been put down by other girls, who said that she was ugly and not good enough. She had even struggled with her grades, as I had. I never knew her pain, only the pain she had caused me. But now she was reflecting her hurt on me and now, as adults, we overcame it together. I forgave her and I can say I truly love this woman as a cherished friend. This brought healing to both of us. Pray for those who persecute you for they are possibly being persecuted as well.

Ephesians 6:11-15 *11 Put on the whole armor of God, so that you may be able to stand against the wiles of the devil. 12 For we wrestle not against flesh and blood, but against principalities, against powers, against the rulers of the darkness of this world, against spiritual wickedness in high places. 13 Wherefore take unto you the whole armor of God, that ye may be able to withstand in the evil day, and having done all, to stand. 14 Stand therefore, having your loins girt about with truth, and having on the breastplate of righteousness; 15 and your feet shod with the preparation of the gospel of peace."*

God gives you everything to arm yourself against the devil, but it is better to flee from the evil we face if all is possible. Karate has taught me to be aware of my surroundings and for those unfortunate times when you must face that evil, to be prepared. This also taught my son that fighting is not the answer, and not to use what he learned against others. This training taught him to be careful, to use little feet where you go, what you do, and speak. My son is a strong, good man today, and I feel that Karate has helped him in his life to stay on a better path. Now we all have rebelled and strayed from our path, and he has some but, got back on track and is still being fashioned by the potter on whose promises I will rely.

It took a few years to get to Black Belt and with each level, I felt more accomplished, and I saw this in the ladies that I trained with. It was as if we all had demons that we were defeating in our walk together. In our walk through this life, I truly believe God uses the ones you least expect to help you grow and overcome. These people and places you encounter are His plan for your path and if you pray for true guidance, He will give it to you. One of the main things I have learned in doing my Karate is how not to fight! It is a little ironic that, you train to fight, even with techniques that could cause fatalities, but when you look at the "true meaning of the path," you realize it teaches preparation, but not to go looking for a fight. Turn from it, if you can, and flee from evil.

Proverbs 3:5-6 *⁰⁵ Trust in the Lord with all thine heart and lean not on thine own understanding. ⁰⁶ In all thy ways, acknowledge Him, and He shall direct thy paths.*

Katrina Putnam:

1ˢᵗ Degree Black Belt: Tae-Kwon-Do

Using the fruits of the spirit as the different Katas, guided our spiritual growth with God and his word, strengthening mental as well as physical strength. For me, this was a great foundation that kept me grounded in my walk with the Lord. I gained physical and spiritual strength in my mind and body. I learned not to fight, by not putting myself in those situations that led me into danger. Gaining the knowledge of how to defend myself if the fight came to me…..."don't go into that dark alley". Where in the Bible does it say to flee from evil?

2 Timothy 2:22*. Flee the evil desires of youth and pursue righteousness, faith, love, and peace, along with those who call on the Lord out of a pure heart.* ***Psalms 34:14*** *Depart from evil, and do good; seek peace, and pursue it. If you daily put on the* ***Full Armor of God*** *you will be protected as David against Goliath, Daniel in the lion's den, and Shadrach, Meshach, and Abednego in the fiery furnace.* ***Ephesians 6: 16-17*** *¹⁶Above all, taking the shield of faith, wherewith ye shall be able to quench all the fiery darts of the wicked. ¹⁷And take the helmet of salvation, and the sword of the Spirit, which is the word of God. Our fight is not with each other but against the evil of this world and the devil who influences it.*

White belt=LOVE

Yellow belt=JOY

Orange belt=PEACE

Green belt=PATIENCE

Purple belt=KINDNESS

Blue belt=GOODNESS

Brown
belt=FAITHFULNES

Red belt=GENTLENESS

Black   belt=SELF-
CONTROL

This is my son, Jonah Putnam, who worked hard on his growth with karate both physically and spiritually. He was able to go as far as his brown belt. He would have obtained his Black Belt, if the Totally Christian Karate school had not relocated to Tennessee. I feel it truly helped to lay a good foundation for his walk. Jesus gave us promises, on which I stand strong, that his word will not return void.

***Isaiah 55:10–11** says, [10] "For as the rain comes down, and the snow from heaven, and do not return there, but water the earth, and make it bring forth and bud, that it may give seed to the sower and bread to the eater, [11] So shall My word be that goes forth from My mouth; it shall not return to Me void, but it shall accomplish what I please, and it shall prosper in the thing for which I sent it.*

Jonah is now a grown man with a good and kind heart who is accomplished in his work. As an adult his path has gotten curvy, but with God's promises, I have faith he will always stand true.

I knew God was real at the age of 5 years old because I had been diagnosed at the age of 3 ½ years with Leukemia. They called it "the baby killer". My parents were able to get me into a research program testing a new drug. This helped them with the cost of my treatments, which came as a real blessing at this time, and helped calm their fears of maybe losing their child. My Daddy did not go to church with us, he would come only on special occasions, such as Christmas, Easter, and other special holidays, but not on Sunday. He did have faith, and believed, and he trusted God could heal his child.

My Daddy took me to a revival, where several ministers prayed over me, and anointed me with oil. You could feel the presence of the Lord in this church and when we went to sit back down, I was so tired, that I laid down on the bench, and suddenly there was a hand on my back. Later, I asked my Daddy if he had put his hand on my back while I was lying there, and he said no, baby, I didn't put my hand on your back. The hand on my back was the hand of Jesus, I know! I went home and told Momma that Jesus had touched me and I was going to be okay. I was cured at the age of 10 years old with no sign of cancer! The doctors could not understand. Yes, I was put in the research study and given the new medication, but the true physician touched me and guided the hands of those who administered the treatments. God's grace and healing touch that cured me, and this is how I know and trust my God is real and alive today.

I was 7 years old when I was saved. It was my Sunday school teacher who helped me to learn who God was and taught me about His son Jesus Christ. My mother was taking me to church before I was born and I had heard about God and Jesus all my life, but by faith I started understanding and developing a knowledge of God's Word at this young age. I wanted to know more and stay strong in my walk and faith. The denomination of the church we went to would teach of "falling from grace" and this thought alone scared me. The more I jumped into God's word, the more I realized that once you are truly His child, no one or anything in this world can snatch you out of his hand.

John 10:29,30 *29 My Father, who gave them Me, is greater than all; and no man is able to pluck them out of My Father's hand. 30 I and my Father are one.*

That gave me not only strength in my walk, but also accountability. My God, Creator of the Universe, Lord of Lords, The Great I Am, knew my name, a sinner, a nothing. What can I offer. Who am I that the Lord of all creation knows my name and wants me in Heaven with Him and sent His Son to die for me.

As I got older, being a Christian got harder. I was influenced by my "friends," my peers, and the things of this world. I thought, "Why should I give up all the fun and freedom this world offers and sit at home when my friends are partaking in the pleasures of this world, and going out to places like bars and night clubs." So, I ran far and fast from the Lord. I partook in all the sins of this world. I was playing a fool's game. I found alcohol and it got a hold on me and the more I drank, the more I wanted it. There was no harm in going to a party with friends and drinking as long as we stayed put and who was I hurting. Well, I found myself in situations I should not be in, and if not for God never leaving me, I would not be alive today. I was hurting myself and my family by acting the way I did, and doing the things I was doing, and influencing others. Yes, I was still God's child, so people were watching me..."She said she was a Christian". But I was not showing Jesus to others. The Lord, being a good Father, never left me although I disappointed Him, and yes He disciplined me, and humbled me. This lead me back to Him, where I should have stayed to begin with. Through God's Sovereign Grace and Mercy, He forgave me, and I re-started my walk. I realized that I must live in this world, but I don't have to be of it. Yes, I struggle daily, and you know Jesus is still with me and His Holy Spirit guides my path. Yes, I have slipped so many times and He is always there to put the pieces back together. I truly believe my experience with Totally Christian Karate helped to build a stronger foundation in my true adult life and the foundation my mother and father and my church helped build helped me to return to God. Although I ran from Him, He never left me, and that can be very humbling. Thank you, Jesus!

I have helped my good friend, James Cooper, as an Assistant Karate Instructor a few times in his classes, and I plan to continue to assist him in the future. My testimony cannot compare to the things my friend James has overcome, and I am blessed to have him as my friend. Our God has a plan, and He puts people in your path for a reason. They maybe there for a short time or a long time, but He has a plan. Trust God's plan for your life and in your walk. It brings me joy to see others accomplish something they can be proud of, and I get to tell them of my Jesus and what he has done for me. To God be the Glory.

Deuteronomy 31:6 *⁰⁶ Be strong and courageous. Do not be afraid or terrified because of them, for the Lord your God goes with you; he will never leave you nor forsake you."*

My Affirmation: My God is bigger, no matter what you face, He is bigger, and can take care of it. David knew this as he faced Goliath, he had faith. So, when you face your giants, remember, "Your God is bigger and keep the faith."

References

1.	https://www.totallychristiankarate.com
2.	Holy Bible, King James Version

Article by....

Avery King – August 19, 2014

Lately, I heard about someone taking photos of the religious quotes and symbols on the wall of our Martial Arts Center, and posting that "this is why people don't come here more". Sensei Ray Rice believes in the Bible and in creationism! You may disagree with him, but what you will learn, is that he is a man who has standards, beliefs, and convictions that he stands for. Our school is the only world class association-backed martial arts program in Rutherford County, NC. The sign above our front door reads, "Mind, Body and Spirit". Most people mistreat their bodies, don't appreciate the power their thoughts have over their life, and many don't even believe in anything spiritual, whether you call it an energy field or whatnot. There is so much to learn here, and it takes a small mind and a blind soul to make something negative out of something so powerful and good. My Sensei spent his life building this. For me, I will keep a state of thankfulness and see what I can learn from those who have "been there and done that." That is my conviction!

Article by....

Karate Magazine

Ray Rice has been active in Marital Arts since 1971 and holds the rank of 8th degree Black Belt. He has also earned belts in Shotokan, Tae-Kwon-Do, Kenpo, Ju-Jitsu, and Akido. He was tested and certified for each rank by a national reputable panel of judges, which included one of his instructors, Steve Lazenby, a 3rd generation Black Belt from the Founder of Shotokan Karate, Gishin Funakoshi, and has also furthered his training in "Kobudo" (martial arts weaponry) with certifications in martial arts weapons.

Ray's martial arts training has been enhanced by many seminars with world renowned "masters" and champions such as Chuck Norris, Bill Wallace, Joe Lewis, Ernie Reyes, Steve Lavalle, Royce Gracie, and more. Ray's statistics as a competitor have gained recognition on national television, as have interviews in several national sport Karate magazines that document his success and demonstrate his well-rounded approach to positive reinforcement as a martial arts instructor.

His sport tournament competition has netted hundreds of wins in Kumite (Fighting), KATA (Empty Hand Forms), Weapons, and the most dominant division, Self-Defense, for which he held the National Competitor of the Year Award for five years.

Ray's personal goals have been accomplished in the kickboxing ring representing Rutherford County (NC) honorably in 18 states in the U.S. and internationally in Canada, France, Italy, and Russia. Early in his career, he earned state titles and then progressed to become the Southeast Title Holder in his weight division and was recognized as one of the top 10 Kick boxers in the world. With over 100 matches in the ring, he held 3 World Titles – the W.K.C. (World Kickboxing Council), and the W.K.F. (World Kickboxing Foundation) Middle Weight Titles of 1992-93-94-95, and the North American Middle Weight Title under the W.K.A. (World Kickboxing Association) and the 1995 – U.S. (Kick) Middle Weight Chap Karate International Council of Kickboxing.

The most important indicators of Rice's success are the students who have become black Belts. With a minimum of 4 years of training, every "active" Black Belt who earns this rank is qualified and capable of contributing to society in a positive way. This program has produced confident, well mannered, and successful leaders in the community.

MY LIFE

I was just a skinny little teenager when I began my first day of teaching Karate in Rutherford County. The date was May 17, 1975, and that first class was the first step toward fulfilling my dream to open a Karate Martial Arts Center. Never could I have

imagined all that I would have to deal with in the years that followed just to keep the school open and my dream alive. The Bible says in John 16:33 that you will have troubles and tribulations, but if you live and walk with God, you can overcome them. Now, looking back over these years, saying that I faced troubles and tribulation seems like an understatement. But my biggest problem was that I failed to walk with God. Although I was a good person, I didn't study His word, pray, or trust in

God completely. As a result, I made a lot of mistakes by not trusting Him and not following His way.

During the late 70's, I lost two very close friends – Rick and Jack – in tragic accidents. Both of these friends had been constant sources of inspiration to me and were partly responsible for helping to keep my goals and dreams for the school alive. I could have been with them in the accidents when they died, but I know God spared my life. Only minutes before, something or someone told me to go the other way. I also realize that God had a plan for my future, and I believe that plan was for me to be a positive influence and to have a Karate program for the people of our county and the surrounding areas.

For the first nineteen years, I worked a second and third job in order to pay the school bills and rent. Even so, I found it very hard to ask for class fees each month. I learned that there were some who knew "Good ol' Ray" would cover it. Some people even looked at the school as a "free" public service. I soon learned this was not the way to run a business and pay the bills.

In the 80's, I was at the top of my game, traveling, fighting, and competing. I ranked among the top ten competitors across the nation and was well on my way to achieving my personal goal of becoming a World Kickboxing Champion, as well as putting little ol' Forest City on the nationwide map. However, my dreams of glory and the big time came screeching to an abrupt halt. Early one Sunday morning,I received a phone call informing me that my school was engulfed in flames. When I arrived at the scene, the building was completely destroyed; my dream lay in smoldering ashes. Previously, some threats had been made, but I was young and had overlooked them (or not taken them seriously). It was just incomprehensible to my mind that a jealous group would go to this extent to hurt me and bring me down. This disaster came just when I was about to go full-time with the school. Because I had no insurance when the school was burned, I had to work for several years on other jobs just to pay for the losses and to start all over again.

A few years later, just when things were coming together for the school again, two of my cars were destroyed, twice our home was broken into and precious things were either stolen or destroyed. Many times, those who were peer pressured by bad angels (influences), broke into the school itself. And I figured there must be an egg shortage in this area because of the number of times the front of the school has been vandalized with eggs.

Some have even tried to ruin my reputation and hurt my family with lies and slander. People whom I rusted and considered my closest friends, have drained us financially. Some days, it was hard for me to go to school and keep a smile on my face. It was especially difficult when people actually believed the lies and judged me accordingly. I was getting crazy with all the junk going on, and I was always wondering what was going to happen next. I felt I couldn't trust anyone.

The Bible says in Rev 12:7, that there was a war in Heaven when Satan challenged God, His Word, and His Love. The Archangel Michael went to battle against Satan and his soldiers and kicked them out of Heaven. During those difficult times, it seemed as if some of those bad angels fell right here in this area. And many did!

I have to believe that those who tried to destroy the school and me were non-believers and those who didn't fit into our program, which emphasizes honor, respect, loyalty, honesty, and builds positive character.

Back in the early 80's, when really bad things were going on, my dad advised me to stop fighting for a while because I had all this bad stuff on my mind. My ability to concentrate was a concern, but I didn't listen to him and as a result, I lost my first fight ever in Oct. 1982. To make matters even worse, this fight was held right here in my hometown, of all places (People still remember that loss. Even though later, I fought the same guy in a re-match and won). That loss and a lot of other things caused me to construct a wall between myself and the world and even between myself and my family and friends. I was afraid they were all fakes and wanted to destroy me, so for years this wall stood. This wall kept everyone from getting close to me. It nearly cost me my family and friends.

During the past few years, when I trusted and financed people to go to seminars on how to grow and staff our school, I found myself used once again. When they quit and I heard the wild stories they were telling, it really hurt. They acted as if they'd get even with me for doing something good. It's hard for me when students who are out of control quit the school, even though I tried to help and discipline them in a positive way. There have been some I believed to be good instructors who left and turned against the school and me; some left the school thinking the grass was greener somewhere else. They later found out they were wrong, but pride kept them from coming back. Many students quit because they said they didn't like the positive stuff in class and later I've seen some of their names in the court news. If only they had stayed with our program! It hurts when you realize you have never taken the time to attend your own son's birthday party because you felt you had to be at the school, because someone might get mad. And when someone is angry with me because someone else made decisions or said things, they have no right to say or do. It hurts to know I can never go out with my family without hearing negative comments about who I am and what I do. It hurts when I've trained others and put my trust in them (many times) in order for them to open schools and programs in other locations, only to discover their false loyalty when they pull my students away from their facility. Each of their ventures has failed. It also hurts when one person turns against our program and then peer pressures others into staying away from my school. But whenever I try to help, it ends up making me the "bad guy". Another issue has been all the recorded messages I've received from jealous and negative callers over the past few years. There are so many other things that I could mention but I just can't bear to write them all down for you to see.

When, finally, in 1990, my dad got me to tear that wall down, I learned that he had only a short time to live. I began to realize how short life is and of all the time that I'd wasted (behind that wall). My dad's death inspired me to pursue my dream of becoming the World Kickboxing Champion once again. People tried to tell me that I was too old, but I was determined, so at thirty-something, I trained countless hours every week, just as I had when I was younger. During this time, I was more focused than I'd ever been in my life. Soon, I was one of the Top Ten Middleweights in the World. Each and every time I stepped into the ring with another world-ranked fighter my dad's words and love were with me. His words strengthened and encouraged me and came from the Bible. An example is Romans 8:30, which asks, "If God is with you, who can be against you?" I was fortunate enough to be recruited and promoted to fight across the United States in sixteen different states, and also in several countries, including France, Italy, Russia, and Canada. Thanks to my dad's help in getting my heart and mind back in line with God, I won my first World Title in 1991, then two other World Titles. I retired undefeated from Kickboxing in 1997.

My strength was further tested when I lost some of my people (family) who were closest to me: Mom in 2005; Dad in 1992;

Stanley in 1994; Jeff in 1996; John in 1997; and Pat in 1998. One of the hardest things in the world I ever had to do was going back in to teach my classes and try to smile on the very same days these loved ones were laid to rest, especially since I never had a day to myself when I could just be free to mourn.

Please don't take me wrong, because I definitely don't want anyone feeling sorry for me. It's just that I hate it when people judge me without knowing the true facts. I hope this will help set the record straight because it is the true facts. I know there is always a price to pay to get ahead or to the top of your game. Often, the price is extremely high, that's why I stay so busy, so I don't have time to stop and think about it.

Okay, I'll stop before I say too much. Let's talk good stuff. That's what keeps me teaching classes every week. I wear many hats, and I love and care for each and every student, no matter how young or old. It makes my day when a child looks up at me with a smile and I feel all that love and care coming back at me. I love to see the delight on a child's face when I give him or her a simple pat on the back and say, "way to go!" That makes it worth it all. Some of the kids have never heard good and loving words in their lives. There are hundreds of testimonies people have written throughout the years expressing how this school has affected their lives in a positive way. At times, I've even been somewhat of a hero to many students by going to their school or workplaces; by listening, talking, and helping with their problems; by giving praise, comforting, caring and backing someone up when nobody else would; by aiding a teacher with a child who has a specific problem; and by doing the best I can to help a child who whispers the unthinkable in my ear and confides in me about what is going on in their life.

Hearing someone say "thanks" for the call or the card and having them tell me, "I didn't think anyone cared"; when a parent looks me in the eye and says "thank you"; when a teenager tells me that Karate has been a positive influence in their life and that it keeps them out of gangs, drugs, and violence; having a student say "thank you" for telling them about Jesus; when someone thanks me for hanging their life; receiving the cards, notes, drawings, gifts of love, the parents' positive comments, as well as the encouragement from community leaders who believe in our school and its program, which teaches Respect, Discipline, Self-Image, and Good Character Building. These are the things that keep me going.

I give thanks for the way my Mom and Dad brought me up, although it almost resembled a boot camp and for the first sixteen years with my Dad. He taught me never to quit anything I started and to give 110% at all times. I also give thanks to God, who brought me to my knees. God already knows ahead of time about the people who will cross paths with me through our program. I thank God for the special characteristics and the perseverance that have given me the will to go on in this short time I'll spend on Earth. Nobody can take that away from me.

I give thanks to all those who stand tall and financially support the program. I give thanks for Matt. 18, which says, "What God has joined together, let no man separate"; for my wife, Anita, who has stood by me during the many bad times I've had; and for my sons Brandon and Cory.

Well, I've got to go for now. I have a new student at the door and it's almost time to start teaching my next class.

I wrote this up in 2000 – Wow, I could write another book since then of the people and things that have come and gone – Anyway,I love and care for each student and parent beyond understanding – Past ~ Present, ~ Future – Never give up or in!

Your instructor and friend forever!

Marty Knight

Born and bred in Belton, SC, Marty Knight is a five-time world champion and three-time national champion with numerous other titles under his black belt, but he didn't begin his athletic career in Karate. Having run track and field in high school, Marty was set to run on scholarship at Anderson College. In the summer prior to his freshman year, he became interested in Karate after seeing the 1971 film Billy Jack. He soon began attending a local Dojo, for fitness and knew right away that he wanted to be a fighter and a teacher.

Mr. Knight would go on to earn his black belt in 1975 while training under Keith Vitali and Mike Genova. He has travelled the world to compete in such countries as Trinidad, China, and was named the most valuable competitor of the Chuck Norris team that traveled to Russia. Additionally, Mr. Knight has served as a bodyguard for well-known entertainment icons including Garth Brooks, Guns N' Roses, and Bon Jovi.

Mr. Knight opened his first karate school in 1978 and has been teaching ever since. His training has produced other world champion fighters such as Rick Lee and Nicki Carlson Lee. In his own words about his profession: "I love my life. I love going to work. I love the lifestyle I lead. It keeps me physically fit and around wonderful people."

In February of 2016, Mr. Knight wouldn't even let a knee replacement surgery keep him off the mats. Coaching from a chair, he continued to drill his students until he was back on his feet again, delivering his famous lightning-fast backfists. Teaching the importance of dedication, diligence, and self-discipline, Marty leads by example and continues to produce champions.

Marty Knight,_an international karate king, was born in Belton, South Carolina. He played all the traditional sports until he was introduced to his lifelong passion, Karate.

Then I went to see a movie called Billy Jack. And we are sitting there watching a movie and the karate in Billy Jack is basic karate, but at the time nobody knew what Karate was. He needed a simple little low kick and kicked this guy in the head, and I am going like, wow. And I sit up in my chair and I watch the rest of the movie. That got me interested in Karate.

After graduating from Belton-Honea Path High School, Marty enrolled in a local Karate class.

From the time he graduated high school to the time I went to college; he was looking for a way to stay in shape besides running around the block. So, he got into Karate. Anderson College offered him a little scholarship to come down and teach Karate in the P.E. Program, as he got his degree. So, he went to Anderson, and the rest was history.

He opened his first Martial Arts school two days after graduating from college.

His mom and dad were totally against his doing Karate because back then, nobody knew what Karate was. And even people he went to college with go like, "What are you going to do for a job?" "I'm going to teach Karate", "Yeah, but what are you going to do for a job?" They thought

Karate was like being a lifeguard during the summer. You know? Well, what are you going to do for a real job? His dad never thought much of it because he did not understand what it was. And his mom, to the day she died, really did not understand what he did in Karate. She knew I ran a Karate studio, but when he got married, she was going, "Oh, that's so good. Cause Bonnie's got insurance." You know, she worried so much about him, not realizing he was making a good living doing Karate. She always worried about him because she thought he was going out, breaking boards with his head, jumping over buildings, and stuff like that. So, he really had no support from them.

Marty pursued a competitive Karate career and went on to win or place in every national tournament. During his professional fighting career, he achieved three national championships and two world titles.

He won between 800-900 of these. And he's not lying to you. The coolest thing about winning a trophy was walking through the airport. In 1985, they rated the top 20 fighters in the nation. No heavyweight, lightweight, nothing, just the top 20 fighters. And he made it in at number 20 and it was like winning the lottery for him.

Because of his national recognition, Marty was asked to join the Chuck Norris Karate team and compete in Russia.

1989, he had just won his first national championship. And he got a call from this guy named Chuck Norris and he said, "Marty, we want you to go to Russia with us and fight on a karate team over there." And in his profession, if Chuck

Norris calls, go. So he went to Russia, and had one of those dream tours. He was there for 16 days (about 2 and a half weeks) and he beat everybody.

Not only has Marty had remarkable success as a fighter himself, but he has also trained numerous national and world champion karate fighters. He has trained more belt women champion fighters than anyone in the history of the sport.

MARTY KNIGHT: On his one record of everybody that he has taught, who has followed in his footsteps and is gone to a national level, there is more success with the girls than the guys. They have won more. I do not know why that is, but there is more success. We say this sport is not gender specific. He had a girl win a 16–17-year-old title two months ago in New York City.

One of his highest honors is being named to the South Carolina Black Belt Hall of Fame. His favorite part is his having taught for so long now that he has instructed people and has instructed their children, and this is no lie. He now has their grandchildren. What better compliment that anybody can say is that I trust you with my family? To say I trust you with my child is a better compliment than saying, Oh, I saw you on ESPN or something like that.

Taking his expertise outside of the studio, Marty and several of his trainees have served as bodyguards for professional entertainers. The list I have had of bodyguards goes from Elton John to George Straight. I mean, everybody. The first guy everybody guarded was a guy named Rick Springfield.

The Eagles came to Clemson. We were body guarding for them. So, they pulled up at two and in the afternoon, to show us, they went up on stage and I had all my people in their place. So, I am just sitting there watching them and they go through every single song that they are going to do in the concert. You

know, they will stop one song and go, "All right, you need to amp that up a little bit." But he had a private concert watching the Eagles. He worked for John Bon Jovi. And he comes out of his dressing room one day and he says, "Come on." So, we go sit on the stage and he gets out his guitar. And he goes through a bunch of songs, and he is sitting right there. And it is him and John Bon Jovi and he is going like, nobody is here to see this? And now he would have cell phones and everything. And he got the bodyguard job for Paul McCartney, who was a Beatle who, when he was your age, was the bomb. So the bodyguard process, he got to meet a lot of people and do a lot of stuff.

This Marshall Arts master remains an advocate for the sport of karate.

With scholarship, people just talk to somebody here at the school. Have them call me. We will scholarship people

From the math of his studio, he continues to shape a new generation of exploring karate enthusiasts.

You always take your chances. They told him that he could never do karate. They told him he could never be a fighter. They told him he did not have the talent. And he was going to, like, watch me. I do not care if I make it or not, but you know, watch me. I am going to try it. So, if you want to be something, be something. If you're going to mess up, make mistakes that is how you learn. I tell a lot of people not to worry about being cool, worry about being good. If you are good at something, you are automatically cool. As far as my life is concerned, I am on my way out as opposed to on my way in. But now what gives me pride is that I can make a difference in a child's life.

Marty once won 126 Tournaments in a row!

www.ingramcontent.com/pod-product-compliance
Lightning Source LLC
Chambersburg PA
CBHW041212150726
48006CB00016B/2214